Bass instruments edition

For Cello, Trombone, and Bass Recorder
plus chords for Guitar & Keyboard

Kevin
Mayhew

We hope you enjoy *A Pocketful of Tunes* for Bass clef instruments.
Further copies of this and the other books in the series
are available from your local music shop.

In case of difficulty, please contact the publisher direct:

The Sales Department
KEVIN MAYHEW LTD
Rattlesden
Bury St Edmunds
Suffolk IP30 0SZ

Phone 01449 737978
Fax 01449 737834

Please ask for our complete catalogue of outstanding Instrumental Music.

First published in Great Britain in 1995 by Kevin Mayhew Ltd

© Copyright 1995 Kevin Mayhew Ltd

ISBN 0 86209 720 7
Catalogue No: 3611176

Cover design by Neil Pinchbeck
Music edited and arranged by Donald Thomson
Music Setting: Tracy Cracknell

Printed and bound in Great Britain

Contents

Arranger's Note

The tunes in this book have been arranged for instruments that read from the Bass clef. Although the melody line may be played alone, accompanying chords for use by keyboard or guitar players have also been provided. Where necessary, an easier version for guitar using a capo is shown below the keyboard chords.

OVER THE SEA TO SKYE

Traditional Scottish Melody

TRUMPET TUNE

Henry Purcell

SPRING from 'THE FOUR SEASONS'
Antonio Vivaldi

KUM BA YAH
Traditional Angolan Melody

DAISY, DAISY
Harry Dacre

AIR from SUITE NO 3 R

Johann Sebastian Bach

WALTZING MATILDA

Marie Cowan

MICHAEL, ROW THE BOAT ASHORE
Traditional Melody

JERUSALEM
Charles Hubert Parry

AMAZING GRACE
Traditional American Melody

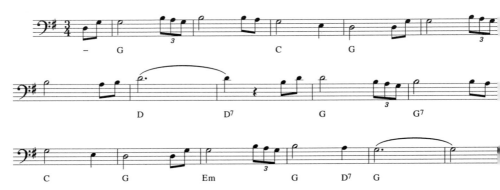

ALL THE NICE GIRLS LOVE A SAILOR
A J Mills and Bennett Scott

GREENSLEEVES
Anonymous 17th Century Melody

RULE, BRITANNIA

Thomas Arne

BLOW THE WIND SOUTHERLY

Traditional English Melody

THE DRUNKEN SAILOR
Sea Shanty

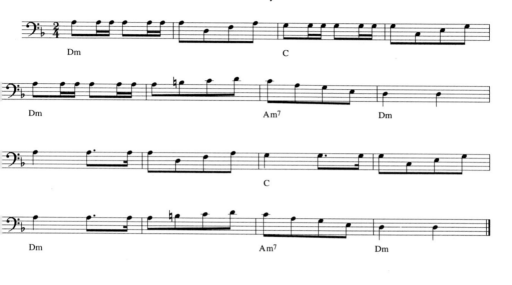

ODE TO JOY
Ludwig van Beethoven

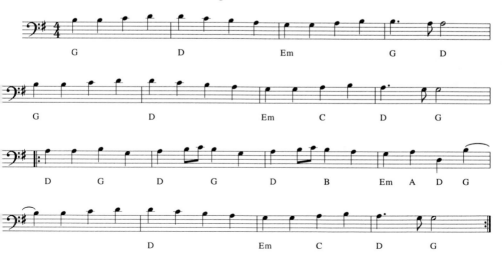

THE KEEL ROW
Traditional English Melody

O SOLE MIO
Eduardo di Capua

SCARBOROUGH FAIR
Traditional English Melody

THE FLOWERS THAT BLOOM IN THE SPRING

Arthur Sullivan

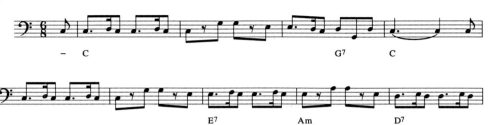

LULLABY

Johannes Brahms

A LIFE ON THE OCEAN WAVE

Henry Russell

COCKLES AND MUSSELS

Traditional Irish Melody

SCÈNE from 'SWAN LAKE'
Peter Ilyich Tchaikovsky

AULD LANG SYNE
Traditional Scottish Melody

THE YELLOW ROSE OF TEXAS

Traditional American Melody

NESSUN DORMA

Giacomo Puccini

WI' A HUNDRED PIPERS

Traditional Scottish Melody

ROMANZA
Anon

Cm   Fm

G   Cm   G   Cm   *Fine*

C   G⁷   C

F   C   G⁷   C   *D.C.*

LITTLE BROWN JUG
R A Eastburn

17

SHAKER SONG
Traditional American Melody

TRUMPET VOLUNTARY
Jeremiah Clarke

RONDO FROM HORN CONCERTO K495

Wolfgang Amadeus Mozart

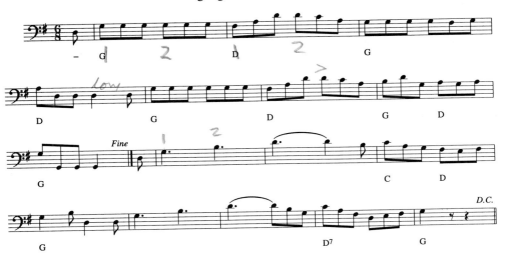

NOBODY KNOWS THE TROUBLE I SEE

Spiritual

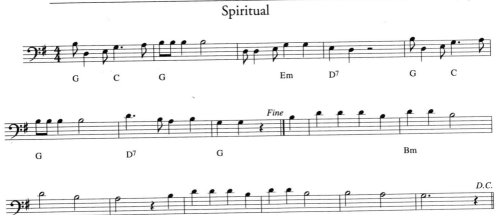

WILLIAM TELL OVERTURE

Gioachino Rossini

THE ENTERTAINER

Scott Joplin

CAPRICE

Nicolo Paganini

ONE FINE DAY from 'MADAME BUTTERFLY'

Giacomo Puccini

BOBBY SHAFTOE

Sea Shanty

PANIS ANGELICUS

César Franck

THE BLUE BELL OF SCOTLAND

Traditional Scottish Melody

HUNGARIAN DANCE NO 5

Johannes Brahms

CLEMENTINE

Percy Montrose

MEN OF HARLECH
Traditional Welsh Melody

TOREADOR'S SONG from 'CARMEN'
Georges Bizet

DANCE OF THE HOURS
Amilcare Ponchielli

LA CUCARACHA
Traditional Mexican Melody

OH DEAR, WHAT CAN THE MATTER BE?
Traditional Melody

DANNY BOY
Traditional Irish Melody

Capo 3

FÜR ELISE
Ludwig van Beethoven

YE BANKS AND BRAES

Traditional Scottish Melody

MANGO WALK

Jamaican Folk Song

PARADE OF THE TIN SOLDIERS
Leon Jessel

THEME from SYMPHONY NO 1
Johannes Brahms

EINE KLEINE NACHTMUSIK

Wolfgang Amadeus Mozart

THE CAN CAN

Jacques Offenbach

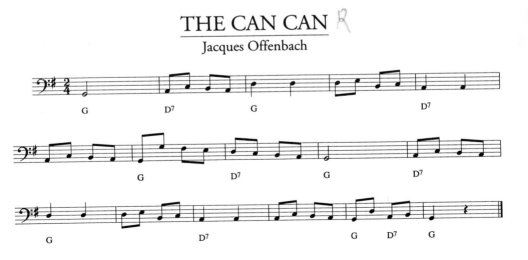

GLORY, GLORY HALLELUJAH
William Stäffe

Capo 3

MORNING HAS BROKEN
Traditional Gaelic Melody

DADDY WOULDN'T BUY ME A BOW-WOW
Joseph Tabrar

SAILORS' HORNPIPE

Sea Shanty

COUNTRY GARDENS

Traditional English Melody

LILLIBURLERO

Traditional English Melody

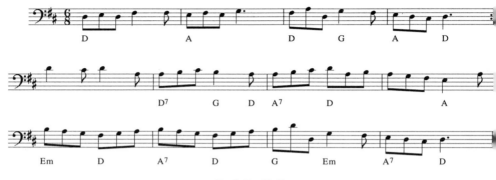

LARGO

George Frideric Handel

THE TROUT QUINTET

Franz Schubert

I DO LIKE TO BE BESIDE THE SEASIDE
John Glover-Kind

PRELUDE
Frédéric Chopin

MY GRANDFATHER'S CLOCK

Henry Clay Work

B♭
A♭
E♭

E♭

Capo 3

EARLY ONE MORNING

Traditional English Melody

Capo 3

I'LL TAKE YOU HOME AGAIN, KATHLEEN
Thomas Westendorf

JOHN PEEL
Traditional English Melody

THEME from VIOLIN CONCERTO

Ludwig van Beethoven

VALSE LENTE from 'COPPÉLIA'

Léo Delibes

GALOP

Jacques Offenbach

DOWN BY THE RIVERSIDE

Spiritual

NEW WORLD SYMPHONY (2nd Movement)

Antonín Dvořák

SHEEP MAY SAFELY GRAZE

Johann Sebastian Bach

AVE VERUM CORPUS

Wolfgang Amadeus Mozart

RADETZKY MARCH
Johann Strauss

⊤ MY BONNIE LIES OVER THE OCEAN
Traditional Melody

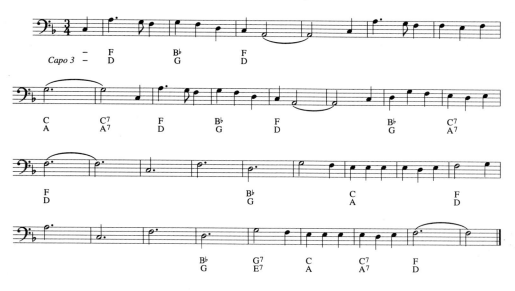

WALTZ
Johannes Brahms

WALTZ from 'DIE FLEDERMAUS'
Johann Strauss

THE ASH GROVE
Traditional Welsh Melody

PROMENADE from
'PICTURES AT AN EXHIBITION'
Modest Musorgsky

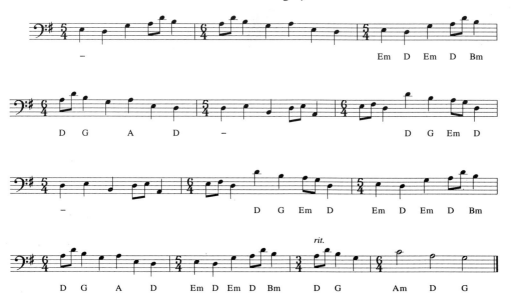

ALL THROUGH THE NIGHT

Traditional Welsh Melody

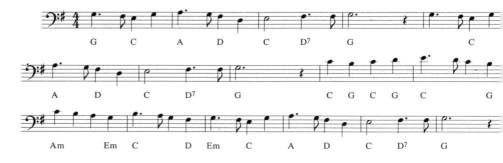

O FOR THE WINGS OF A DOVE

Felix Mendelssohn

THE LINCOLNSHIRE POACHER

Traditional English Melody

O MY BELOVED FATHER
Giacomo Puccini

PAVANE
Gabriel Fauré

POLLY-WOLLY-DOODLE

Traditional American Melody

CHARLIE IS MY DARLING

Traditional Scottish Melody

WHEN THE SAINTS GO MARCHING IN

Spiritual

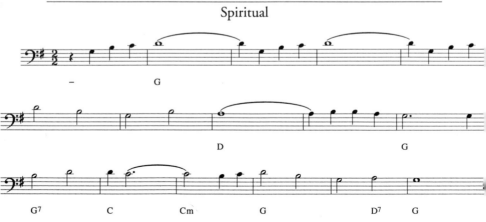

LA DONNA È MOBILE

Giuseppe Verdi

THE FLORAL DANCE

Traditional English Melody

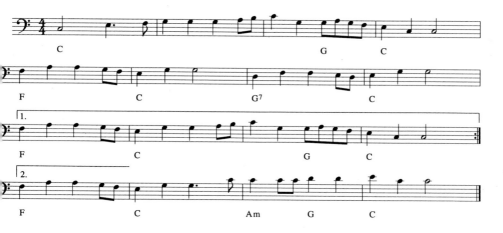

BLUE DANUBE WALTZ

Johann Strauss

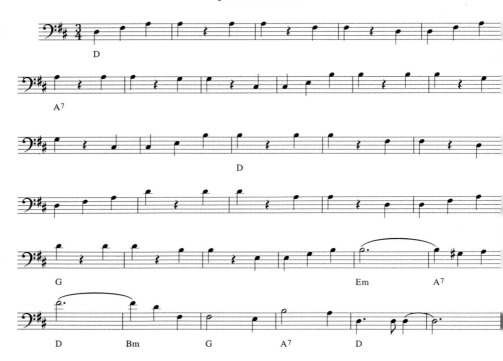

FOR HE'S A JOLLY GOOD FELLOW

Traditional English Melody

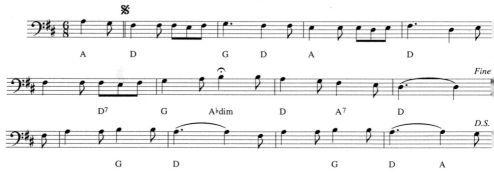

IT'S A LONG WAY TO TIPPERARY
Jack Judge and Harry Williams

LOCH LOMOND
Traditional Scottish Melody

ABIDE WITH ME

William Henry Monk

SWING LOW

Spiritual

GOODNIGHT, LADIES

Traditional English Melody